KNOW YOUR SPORT

Swimming

Paul Mason

W
FRANKLIN WATTS
LONDON • SYDNEY

First published in 2008 by
Franklin Watts
338 Euston Road
London NW1 3BH

Franklin Watts Australia
Hachette Children's Books
Level 17/207 Kent Street
Sydney NSW 2000

Series editor: Jeremy Smith
Art director: Jonathan Hair

Series designed and created for Franklin Watts by Painted Fish Ltd.
Designer: Rita Storey
Editor: Nicola Edwards
Photography: Tudor Photography, Banbury

A CIP catalogue record for this book is available from the British Library.

Dewey classification: 797.2
ISBN: 978 0 7496 7839 5
Printed in China

Franklin Watts is a division of Hachette Children's Books, an Hachette Livre UK company.

Note: At the time of going to press, the statistics and player profiles in this book were up to date. However, due to some players' active participation in the sport, it is possible that some of these may now be out of date.

Picture credits
istock pp 9 and 24; Getty Images pp 6, 10, 15, 19, 25 and 27.

Cover images: Tudor Photography, Banbury.

All photos posed by models.
Thanks to Matthew Corbett, Rashid Olubaji and Emily Page.

The Publisher would like to thank Bloxham School and coaches Sue Corbett and Denise Langford for their help.

Taking part in sport is a fun way to get fit, but like any form of physical exercise it has an element of risk, particularly if you are unfit, overweight or suffer from any medical conditions. It is advisable to consult a healthcare professional before beginning any programme of exercise.

Contents

What is Swimming?

Swimming is one of the world's most popular sports. Some people swim for fun, others in competitions. The very best swimmers are professionals, and have earned millions of pounds from their success.

Swimming Strokes

Different swimming techniques are called 'strokes'. The most popular stroke used to be breaststroke. Breaststroke is easy to learn, but slow. Racers wanted to find something faster. Then, in the 1870s, a swimmer called John Trudgen copied a stroke used by American Indians. It became known as the Trudgen Crawl, which turned into today's front crawl.

Today, the four main swimming strokes are (in order of speed): front crawl, butterfly, backstroke and breaststroke.

The First Competitions

Swimming competitions have been held for thousands of years. From ancient Greece and ancient Rome to Japan, swimming was considered to be an important skill. The winners of races were as famous then as great swimmers like Ian Thorpe are now.

Domenico Fioravanti of Italy celebrates his gold medal win with bronze medallist and Italian team mate Davide Rummolo.

These swimmers are getting advice from their coach.

Swimming Today

Today, competitive swimming is popular at several different levels. The most basic swimming competition is a race between friends at the local pool. Local swimming clubs also hold contests, and regions and even countries all compete against others.

Swimming is now more popular than ever before. Part of the reason is that almost anyone can take part. Even people who find it hard to move around on land can often swim unaided. Whatever shape or size they are, strong or weak, fat or thin, most people can enjoy swimming.

Open-water Swimming

Open-water swimming takes place in large, natural areas of water such as lakes and the sea. Open-water swimming races are increasingly popular, but many people prefer to challenge themselves with a long-distance swim alone. The most famous example is swimming the English Channel.

Swimming at the Olympics

Swimming is a sell-out event at the Olympic Games, the world's biggest sporting competition. At the very first modern Olympics, which were held in Athens in 1896, swimming was one of just nine sports. It has been part of the Olympics ever since. Becoming an Olympic racer takes years of hard work and dedication, and hours of training every day. The rewards for success are huge, though. Ian Thorpe, one of the best swimmers of recent years, became a teenage millionaire because of his swimming success.

Daylight Ban

In Australia, swimming in the sea used to be banned during daylight hours. It was said to be immodest. The ban lasted from 1838 until 1902.

Swimming Basics

Swimming is a very simple sport. All you need is a swimming costume, a towel and some water. There are other pieces of equipment that can help swimmers improve their stroke and get faster.

hat
goggles

Swimming Clubs and Coaches

Most people are taught to swim by their parents, or by an instructor at their local pool. Anyone who wants to get better at swimming, and perhaps take part in races, needs to join a swimming club. Almost all pools have a swimming club that meets there regularly for training. Swimming clubs have a coach or coaches to give swimmers advice on technique, and train them to be fitter and faster.

Equipment

Most competitive swimmers have more than just a costume and towel in their kit bag. They also have:

- Goggles, which stop your eyes getting red and sore, and let you see underwater. Being able to see underwater is very important if you want to improve your technique.
- A rubbery hat, which stretches over your hair. Anyone with long hair needs a hat to keep their hair from going over their eyes.
- A kick-board, which is a float that you can hold on to while swimming along. This makes it

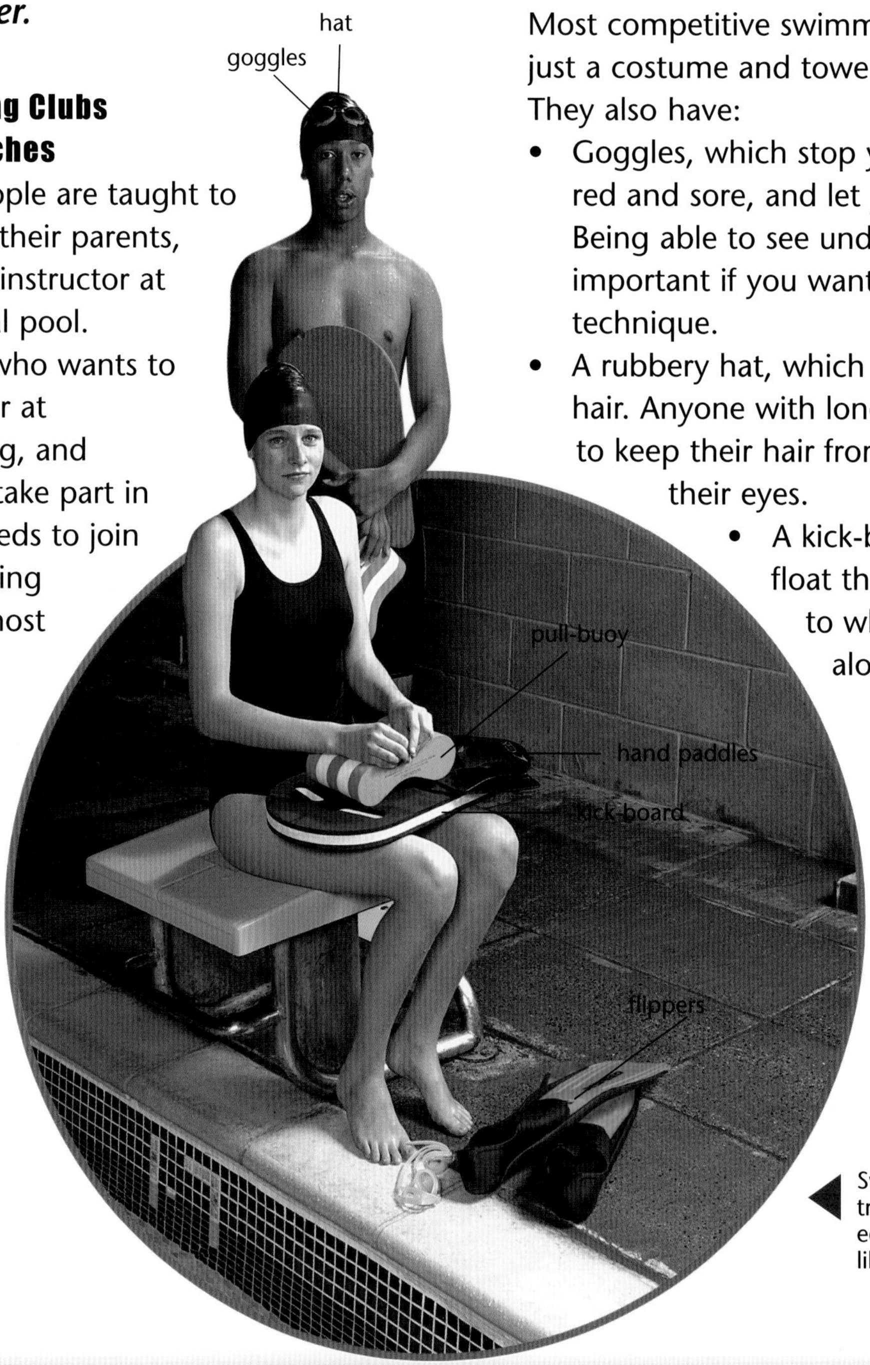

pull-buoy
hand paddles
kick-board
flippers

Swimmers ready for training, with all the equipment they are likely to need.

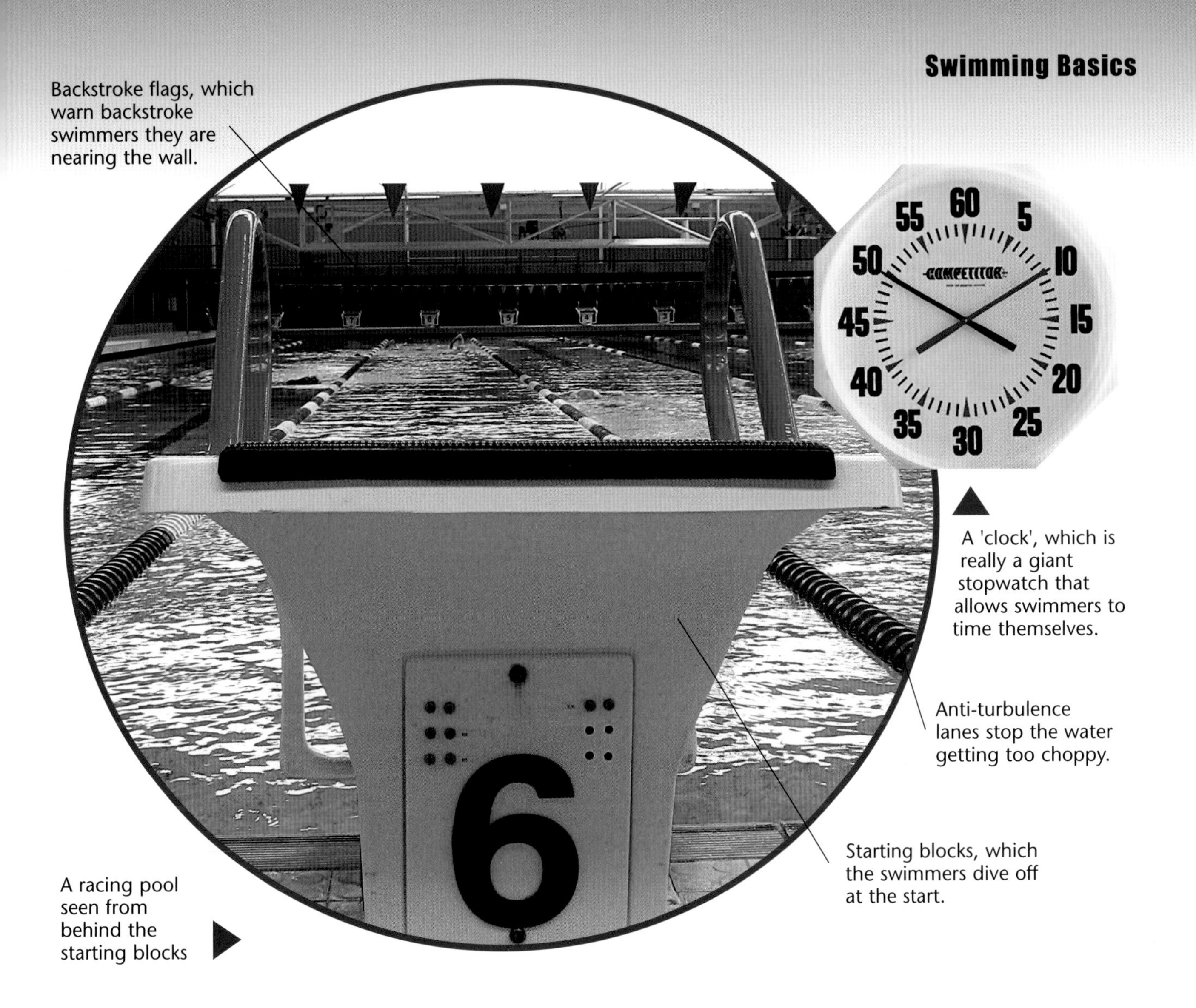

A racing pool seen from behind the starting blocks

possible to practise your leg kick on its own, without doing an arm stroke as well.

- A pull-buoy, which is a float that you tuck between your legs. Using a pull-buoy makes it possible to practise your arm stroke on its own.
- For competitions, swimmers also take a tracksuit and flip-flops to wear between races.

Suits for Speed

During races, some swimmers wear costumes made out of material that is designed to help them go faster. The material creates a thin layer of air bubbles, and the bubbles help the swimmer glide through the water more easily. The costumes work so well that almost all top racers use them. Unfortunately, they are so expensive that very few ordinary swimmers can afford them!

Open-air Swimming

In the past, most people went swimming in rivers, lakes or the sea. Some swimming holes in rivers were so busy that they had their own lifeguards!

Training

Swimming is a great way to get fit. It uses most of the body's muscles. Swimmers are less likely to get injured than some other athletes. The water cushions their bodies and prevents any hard impacts.

Swimming Muscles

Swimming hard gives your body a great workout. Almost every muscle is used. Some muscles are more important than others, though. Top-level swimmers usually have big shoulders and wide backs. These give them a strong arm stroke. They have strong thigh muscles, for a powerful leg kick. Swimmers try to avoid building up their muscles too much, though. They need to stay slim enough to slip easily through the water.

Fitness and Strength

Fitness is the ability to carry on doing exercise for a long time. In competitions, sportspeople nearly always go slower as the race goes on. The fitter they are, they less they slow down. Fitness is important for all swimmers, but especially for those who compete in long-distance races.

Amanda Beard

Date of birth: October 29th, 1981

Nationality: American

Amanda is one of the U.S.A's top swimmers, and a notoriously hard trainer. She first won a U.S. national title in 1995, and was in the team for the 1996 Atlanta Olympics – three years before she finished school! Amanda was also an Olympian in 2000 and 2004, and her achievements include:

- **1996 Olympics: silver in the 100m and 200m breaststroke, gold in the medley relay.**
- **2000 Olympics: bronze in the 200m breaststroke.**
- **2003: sets world 200m breaststroke record.**
- **2004 Olympics: gold in the 200m breaststroke.**

Amanda Beard wins the 200m breaststroke gold medal at the Athens Olympics in 2004.

Swimmers also have to build up strength, or power, in their muscles. If they need to sprint, having strong muscles will allow them to power through the water.

Technique

However fit and strong you are, it is impossible to be a fast swimmer unless you also have good technique. Good swimming technique allows you to swim without using up energy unnecessarily. Every bit of effort helps you to move forwards through the water. The best way to develop your technique is to work with a good coach.

Stretching and Flexibility

Swimmers need bendy, or flexible, bodies for some techniques. In butterfly, for example, they need flexible shoulders. In breaststroke, a flexible lower back is important. Good swimmers warm up their muscles by stretching before they go into the water.

Stretches

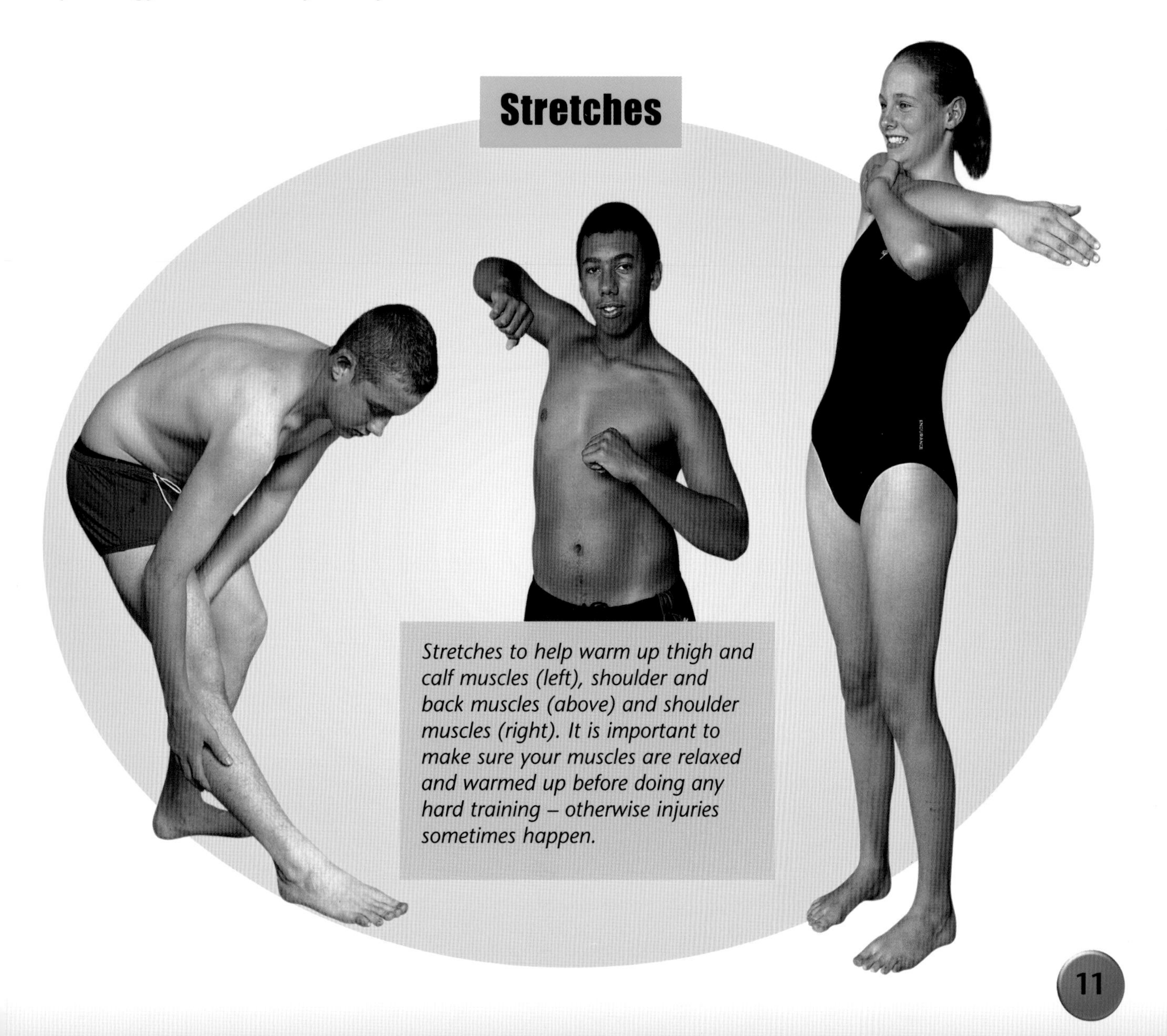

Stretches to help warm up thigh and calf muscles (left), shoulder and back muscles (above) and shoulder muscles (right). It is important to make sure your muscles are relaxed and warmed up before doing any hard training – otherwise injuries sometimes happen.

Breaststroke

Breaststroke is the first stroke many people learn. Until the late 1800s (see pages 6-7) it was almost the only stroke anyone swam. People often kept their faces out of the water as they swam, which made them look a bit like watchful frogs.

Breaststroke Technique

Today, breaststroke technique has changed radically. People who don't want to get their hair wet may still prefer the watchful-frog technique – but coaches now encourage swimmers to dip their face into the water during each stroke. Modern techniques such as this have allowed breaststroke race times to tumble.

Breaststroke

1 *The arm stroke begins with the swimmer's hands moving out and back. The outwards movement lifts the swimmer's body up, and the backwards movement gives speed. At this point the swimmer's legs are still trailing behind.*

2 *The swimmer's hands and arms pull in towards the body. Pulling too far back slows you down – to help stop this happening, many swimmers pull inwards when they can't see their hands in their goggles any more. The swimmer's elbows come in at the bottom of her ribs. At the same time, the swimmer's feet are being drawn back towards her bottom, ready to do a kick.*

Gliding and Timing

Gliding along below the surface and then rising back up again are the things that give breaststroke its speed. Timing your stroke right is the key to swimming breaststroke well. The basic timing is to glide forwards with your face in the water after a kick, then use an arm stroke to lift your body up and forwards, ready for another kick.

3 *The kick finishes, with the swimmer's toes pointing backwards and her feet together. By now the swimmer's head has dropped back into the water and her arms are nearly at full stretch.*

3a *As the next kick starts, the swimmer's hands begin to push forwards. Her head and shoulders begin to drop back towards the water.*

4 *Now the swimmer is making a long, streamlined shape in the water. Her arms are stretched out in front and her legs are stretched out behind. For a couple of heartbeats, the swimmer glides forwards. Then, before losing too much speed, the next arm stroke begins.*

Front Crawl

Front crawl races are technically called 'freestyle', which means you can swim any stroke you like. But because front crawl is fastest, that's the stroke almost everyone uses.

Front Crawl Technique

In front crawl, first one arm pulls, then the other. The legs keep up a constant kicking technique. Swimmers roll their bodies from side to side, but keep them straight in the water.

Breathing

The aspect of front crawl that learners find hardest to get right is knowing when to breathe. Some people find they can only breathe on one side, which is called lateral breathing. They usually breathe every two or four arm strokes. Other people breathe on both sides, which is called bilateral breathing. They breathe every three arm strokes.

Leg Kicks

Front crawl swimmers have a choice of how often to kick their legs:

- Twice every two arm strokes, which is called a two-beat kick.
- Four times every two arm strokes, a 'four-beat kick'.
- Six times every two arm strokes, a 'six-beat kick'.

A six-beat kick is best for short sprints. The others are best for longer distances.

Front Crawl

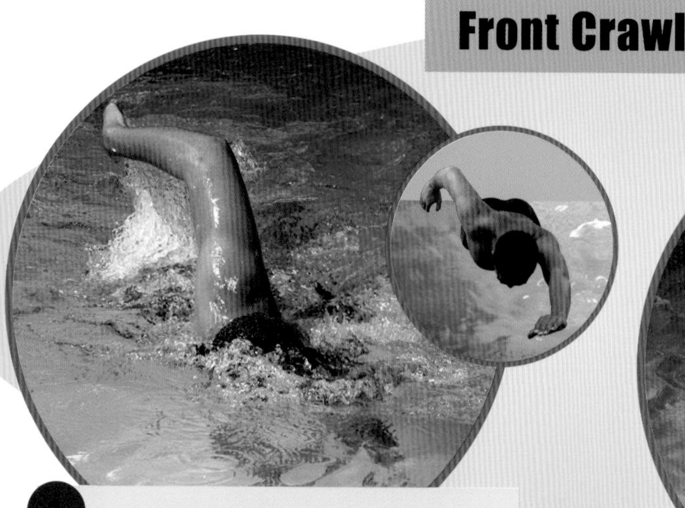

1 *As the left arm stretches forwards, the swimmer's right arm lifts out of the water, elbow first.*

As the swimmer's left arm starts its pull, his right arm lifts free of the water and his hand swings out to the side.

2 *As the swimmer's right elbow reaches its highest point, his hand comes level with his armpit. The left arm continues its stroke.*

Ian Thorpe

Date of birth: October 13th, 1982

Nationality: Australian

Ian Thorpe is probably the best swimmer of modern times. Nicknamed 'The Thorpedo' and 'Flipper', he specialized in the 200m and 400m front crawl. Thorpe first hit the headlines in 1998, at the age of 16, by winning two gold medals at the World Championships. This made him the youngest world champion ever. His other achievements include:

- In 1999, breaking four world records in four days.
- Winning three gold medals at the Sydney Olympics in 2000.
- At the 2001 World Championships, winning six gold medals.
- Holding world records for 200m, 400m and 800m front crawl.

▲ Ian Thorpe helps the Australian team to victory in the 4 x 100m freestyle at the Sydney Olympics in 2000.

3 *Now the swimmer's right arm enters the water, with the elbow bent. At the same time, his left arm is almost finishing its stroke, and is just about to come out of the water near his hips.*

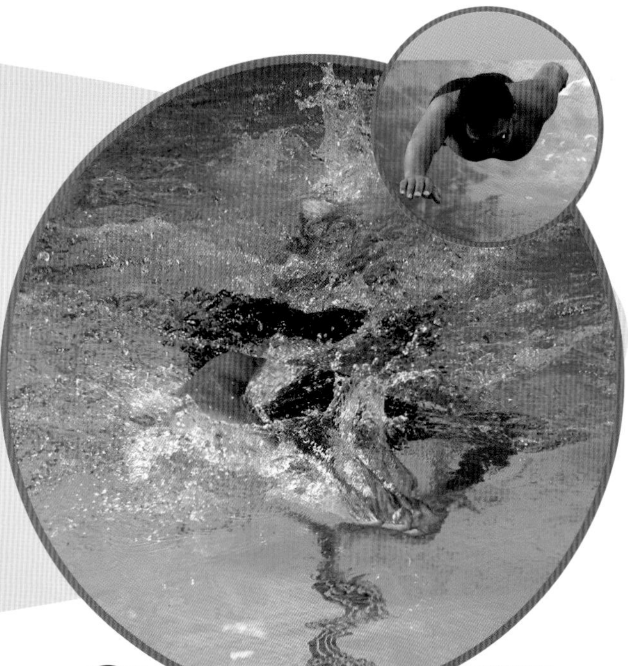

4 *The left-arm stroke is finished, and the right arm is stretched forwards ready to begin a new stroke.*

Backstroke

Many people find backstroke hard to learn because they can't see where they're going. Experienced backstroke swimmers learn to use their surroundings to navigate their way up and down the pool.

Backstroke Navigation

Two things that can help you swim backstroke in a straight line are:

- Using the roof as a guide. Pool roofs often have lines running up and down them in the same direction as the lanes of the pool. Following these means you swim in a straight line.
- Swimming near to the anti-turbulence ropes. This keeps you going straight – but be careful not to get snagged up in them.

The next challenge is knowing if you are about to crash your head into the end of the pool. For training or racing, pools string 'backstroke flags' across the pool. These are always the same distance from the end, so it always takes the same number of strokes from the moment you go under the flag to reach the edge of the pool.

Backstroke

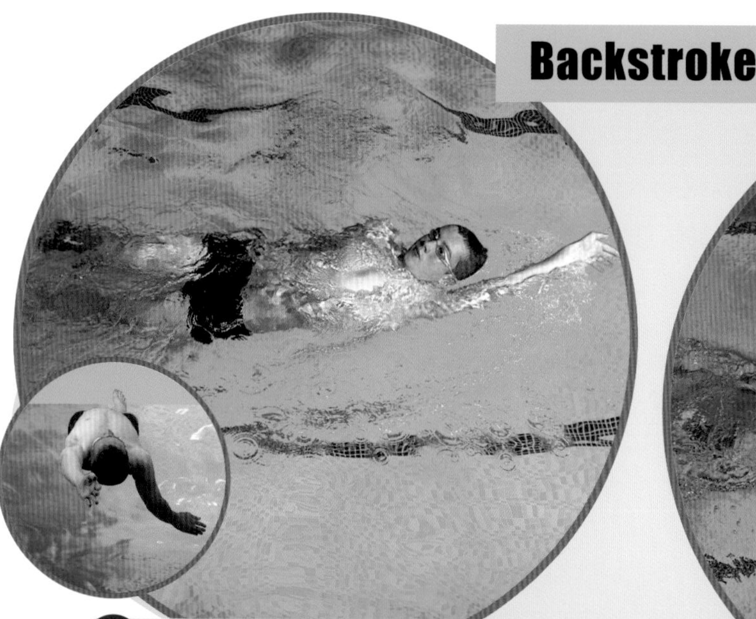

1 *The swimmer's left arm enters the water, with the hand twisted so that his little finger goes in first. His right arm is just finishing its stroke.*

2 *The swimmer's right arm bends slightly and begins to sweep out and back. This drives his body forwards when his left arm lifts out of the water. It is important to keep your body and legs in a straight line and your head still, as this gives a smooth, speedy stroke.*

Backstroke Technique

Backstroke is similar to front crawl. First one arm pulls, then the other. At the same time, the legs keep up a constant kick. Good backstroke swimmers roll their bodies from side to side to move their arms into the water. They always keep a straight path in the water, though.

Bauer's Backstroke

In 1922, Sybil Bauer of the USA became the first woman to beat a men's world record for swimming. She swam a time of 6:24.8 for the 440 yards backstroke.*

***This time was never confirmed as a world record because it had been swum at an unsanctioned meet.**

3 *Halfway through the stroke, the swimmer's left arm is bent so that it is roughly parallel with the surface of the water. His right arm is halfway through the air.*

4 *Now the left arm starts to sweep back in towards the swimmer's hip. Meanwhile, the right arm is about to enter the water.*

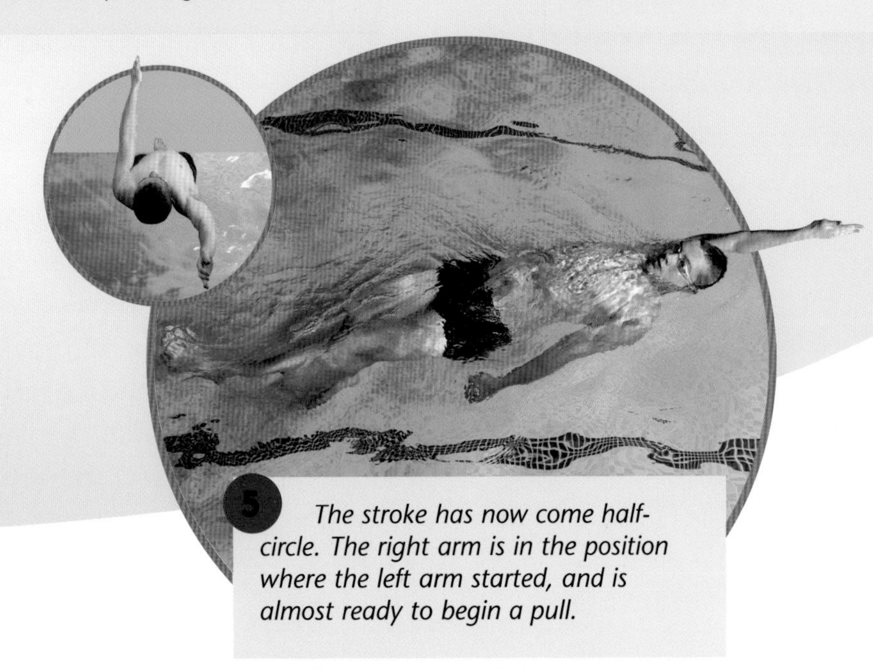

5 *The stroke has now come half-circle. The right arm is in the position where the left arm started, and is almost ready to begin a pull.*

Butterfly

1 *The swimmer's arms drive forwards, then drift to about shoulder width apart as he glides for a heartbeat. As the swimmer's arms begin to pull out and back, his legs begin a kick.*

2 *The swimmer's arms sweep in and then out again, leaving the water as his elbows lift up and forwards. His arms swing out sideways, with the elbows slightly higher than the arms.*

Many people find butterfly the trickiest stroke to learn. Once you get it right, though, swimming butterfly feels as though you are skimming along the surface of the water like a dolphin.

Body Position

People often try to learn butterfly by doing an exaggerated up and down snaky movement with their body. In fact, the fastest way to swim butterfly is to position your body as flat as possible in the water. To breathe, you simply lift your chin forwards, so that your face comes out of the water.

The Dolphin Kick

The butterfly kick is often called a dolphin kick. It is done with the feet and legs together. Swimmers move their hips up and down to send a wavelike movement down their legs. Each arm stroke has two kicks. The first happens when the swimmer's arms go into the water, and the second as they come out. Many swimmers find it easier to do one big kick and one little one.

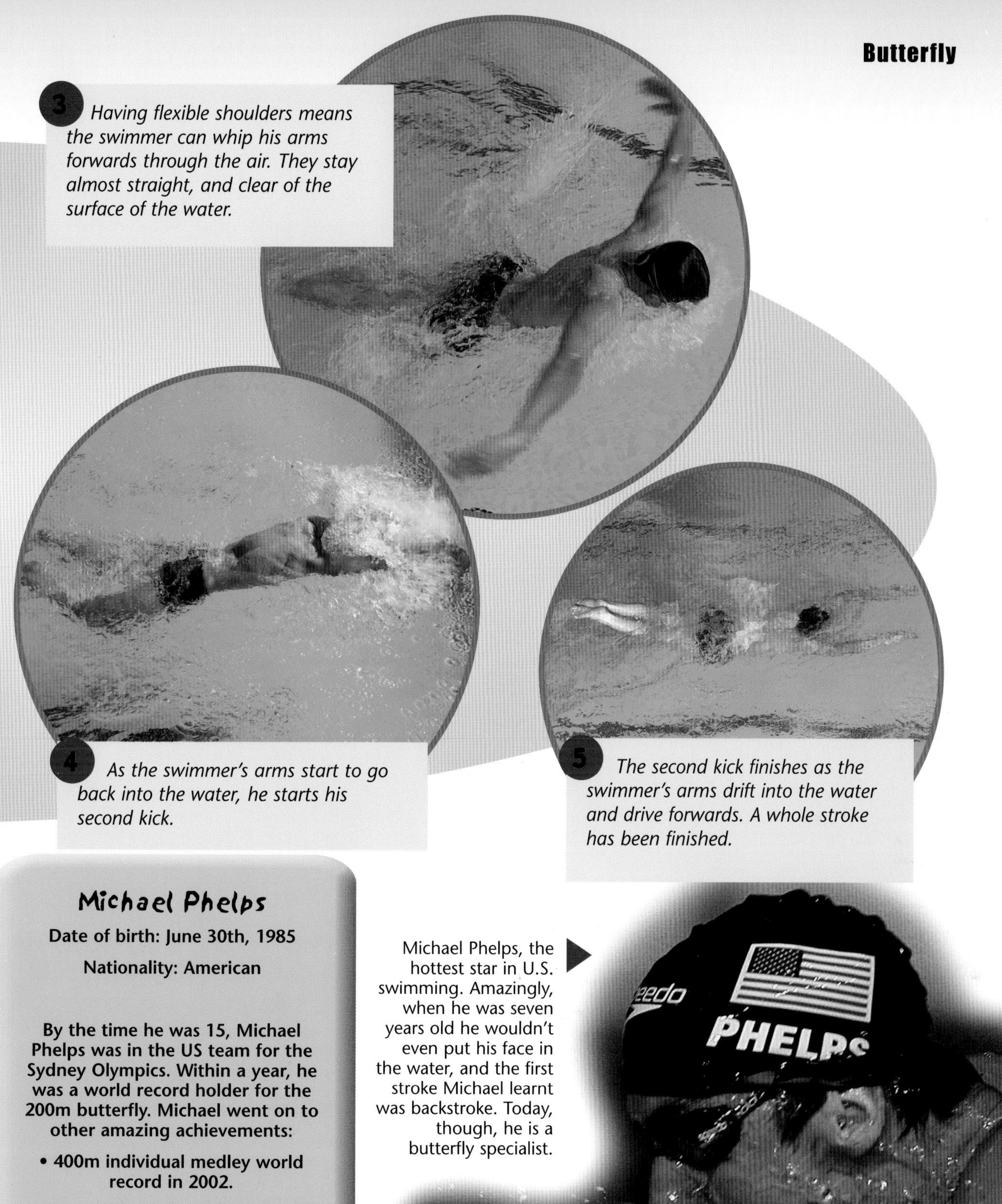

3 *Having flexible shoulders means the swimmer can whip his arms forwards through the air. They stay almost straight, and clear of the surface of the water.*

4 *As the swimmer's arms start to go back into the water, he starts his second kick.*

5 *The second kick finishes as the swimmer's arms drift into the water and drive forwards. A whole stroke has been finished.*

Michael Phelps

Date of birth: June 30th, 1985

Nationality: American

By the time he was 15, Michael Phelps was in the US team for the Sydney Olympics. Within a year, he was a world record holder for the 200m butterfly. Michael went on to other amazing achievements:

- **400m individual medley world record in 2002.**
- **Graduating from high school in 2003, then setting five world records and winning six medals at the World Championships.**
- **In the 2004 Olympics, winning six gold medals and one bronze.**

Michael Phelps, the hottest star in U.S. swimming. Amazingly, when he was seven years old he wouldn't even put his face in the water, and the first stroke Michael learnt was backstroke. Today, though, he is a butterfly specialist.

Dives

Basic dives are great fun for everyone. For racers, though, they are also a way of gaining on opponents whose dives aren't as good. Having a good dive can be the difference between winning and coming second.

Diving Well

In a good dive, the swimmer goes into the water making hardly a splash. It looks almost as though he or she has dived through a tiny, body-sized hole in the surface. The only splash is a little 'plop!' as the diver's feet disappear underwater.

Shallow and Deep Dives

In competitions, swimmers have to choose how deep their dives are going to be. Too deep and they will be drifting underwater for too long, still coming to the surface as the others race off down the pool. Too shallow and they will come to the surface

Starting a Race

1 *The referee blows short blasts on a whistle, then one long one. The long blast is the signal to get on to the starting block.*

2 *Lean forward, ready to step to the front of the starting block. The starter says, "Take your marks," the signal to get into the starting position. The next thing the racers hear is the bang of a starting gun or an electronic beep, signalling that they can dive in.*

Dive Safely

Never dive in unless you are sure:

- The water is deep enough.
- There is nothing you could hit your head on.

As the racers enter the water, arching their backs decides how deep their dive will be. Here, the racer on the left has a more arched back, and will do a shallower dive.

too soon, and end up having to swim further than everyone else. In general, shallow dives are best for front crawl and butterfly. Slightly deeper dives are good for breaststroke.

The Racing Dive

Leap out and away from the side of the pool. Don't worry about leaping out a long way before you hit the water – the shape your body makes as it goes into the water is much more important than how far out you go.

Bend at the waist so that your hands and arms point down towards the water. Keep your head tucked in. Your arms, head and body enter the water in a straight line, as if they are all going through the same tiny hole in the water.

As your hips go into the water, arch your back slightly. The more you arch your back, the shallower the dive will be.

Glide underwater until you have slowed down almost to swimming speed. If the dive was the right depth, you should just be coming to the surface, ready to start swimming.

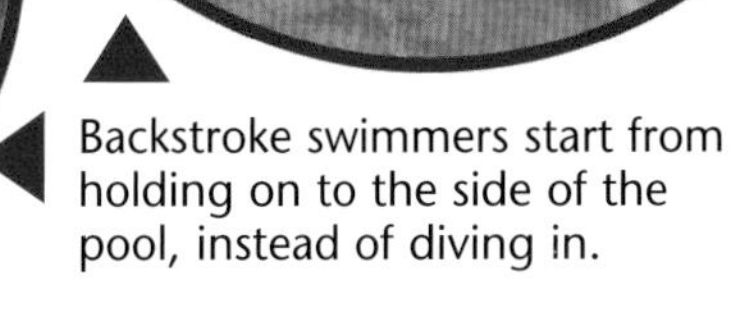

Backstroke swimmers start from holding on to the side of the pool, instead of diving in.

Turns

Like dives, turns give expert swimmers a chance to gain ground on their opponents. Good swimmers can gain two metres on one turn, so for racers they are well worth practising.

Breaststroke Turns

In a breaststroke turn, the swimmer's hands have to touch the wall at the same time and at the same height. After turning and pushing off the wall, breaststroke racers are allowed to do one arm stroke and one leg kick underwater before they come to the surface. Some people can manage 12 metres or more underwater.

Butterfly Turns

Butterfly turns are very similar to breaststroke turns, but there is no limit on how many kicks the swimmer can do underwater. Instead, they have to come to the surface within 15 metres.

Tumble Turns

Tumble turns are the fastest way to turn round when you get to the end of the pool. Front crawl and backstroke racers use tumble turns. Backstroke swimmers turn on their fronts just as they reach the end of the pool. They have to push off on their back, not their front.

Swimmers who can perform good tumble turns can gain a body length on slow-turning rivals.

Breaststroke and Butterfly Turns

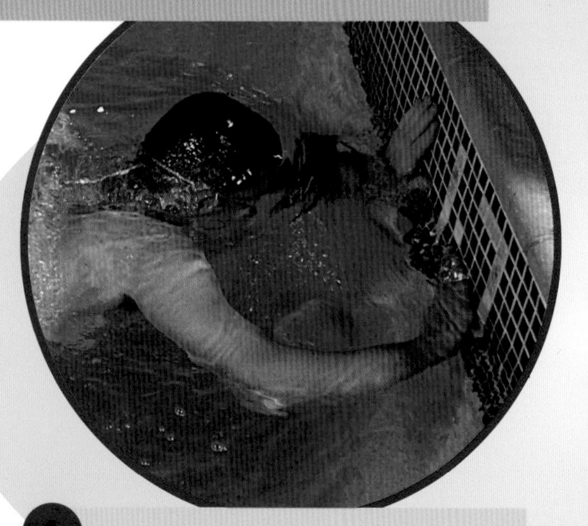

1 *For breaststroke and butterfly, the swimmer's hands have to touch the wall at the same time, right next to each other.*

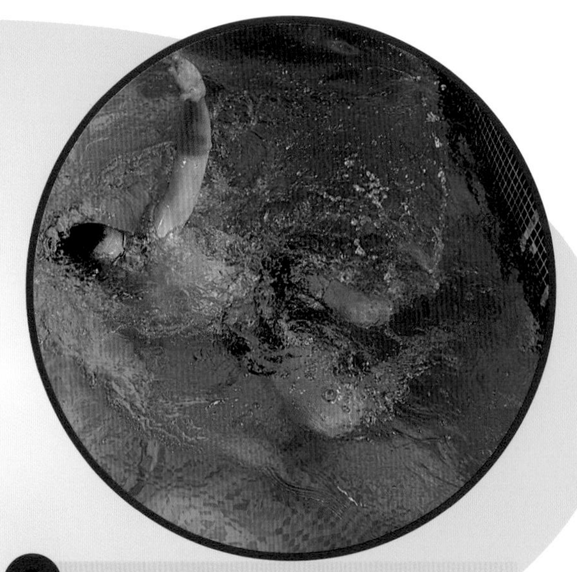

2 *The swimmer then drops one shoulder backwards, pushing against the wall with the other arm to twist his body into position, ready to push off the wall with his feet.*

Tumble Turns

1 About one stroke away from the wall, the swimmer finishes her last arm stroke. One arm is by her side, the other out in front.

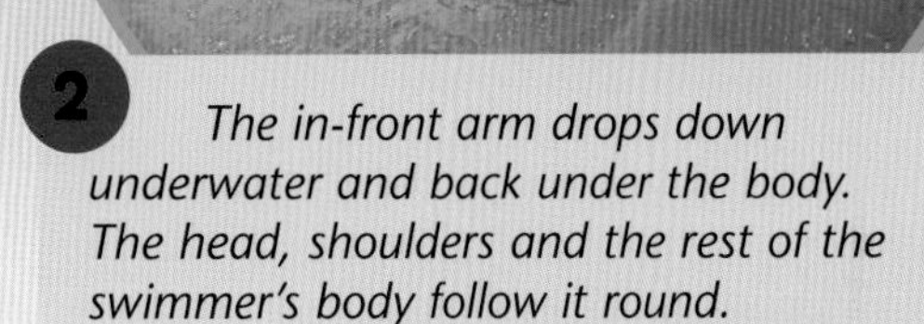

2 The in-front arm drops down underwater and back under the body. The head, shoulders and the rest of the swimmer's body follow it round.

3 Next the swimmer's feet flip over and stop against the wall. Most swimmers have twisted on to their side at this point, though some have turned over completely.

4 The swimmer gives a strong push away from the wall with her legs, twisting on to her front. She keeps a streamlined shape, with arms and legs stretched out for the glide away from the turn.

Racing Underwater

Before the rules were changed, Russian swimmer Denis Pankratov broke several world records for 50m butterfly by swimming the whole race underwater!

Competitions

Taking part in a competition is a good way to judge how much your swimming is improving. Swimmers find out if they can get close to or beat their personal best time, or PB.

Galas and Meets

Swimming competitions are called 'galas' or 'meets'.

• Galas: competitions between teams
The teams may be members of the same club, or from the same area or country. In team competitions, there are points for first, second and third place, and so on, in each race. The team with the most points at the end of the gala wins.

• Meets: swimming championships
In championship meets, swimmers represent their team, but are entered as individuals. There is no adding-up of points at the end, although sometimes teams add up the number of medals they won, as a way of seeing who has done best.

How Competitions Work

Most swimming competitions follow the same routine. First of all there is a warm-up session, usually about an hour before the racing begins. Then the pool is cleared, and the swimmers sit with their teammates, wearing tracksuits to keep warm. When the competition starts, the team manager lets each swimmer know when it is time to go up for their event.

◀ Waiting for the starter to say, "Take your marks!" at the beginning of a backstroke race.

Registration

At swimming championships, individual swimmers let the officials know that they are there and ready to swim by handing in a registration card. The card carries details of the swimmer's entry time (the fastest time they have swum that year).

Heats, Semi-finals and Finals

In a big championship there will be lots of swimmers in each event. For example, there might be 80 entries in the 100m freestyle. Only eight people can swim at a time, so there will be ten qualifying races, called heats. The swimmers with the slowest entry times go in the first heats, the fastest entry times go in the last. The 16 swimmers who are fastest in the heats get through to the semi-finals, and the fastest eight from the semi-finals go into the final.

Major Competitions

The biggest swimming competitions are the World Championships, which take place every year, and the Olympic Games, which happen every four years.

Odd Olympic Races

At the 1900 Paris Olympics, there were two races that would surprise spectators today. The first was an underwater obstacle course, at the bottom of the River Seine! The second was an underwater race without obstacles.

Slow-starting as usual, 'Lethal Leisel' Jones dives in at the start of a 100m breaststroke

Leisel Jones

Date of birth: August 30th, 1985

Nationality: Australian

Despite being famous for her slow starts (she is almost always the last person to dive in), Leisel Jones is so fast at 100m and 200m breaststroke that the Australian press has given her the nickname 'Lethal Leisel'! She is one of the world's top swimmers:

- **Silver medalist in the 100m breaststroke at the 2000 Olympics, when she was just 14.**
- **Bronze in the 100m and silver in the 200m breaststroke at the 2004 Olympics.**
- **World record holder for both 100m and 200m breaststroke.**

Competition Events

Swimming competitions include a big variety of events. There are almost 20 different individual events, and relays as well. It's no wonder that swimming takes up most of the first week at the Olympics!

Strokes and Medleys

There are races over different distances in all four strokes: freestyle (when swimmers almost always do front crawl), backstroke, breaststroke and butterfly.

As well as these, there are individual medley races, where the swimmers swim each stroke in the order butterfly, backstroke, breaststroke, front crawl. Medleys are usually swum over 200m or 400m. The 400m medley is one of the toughest races in swimming. Just as the swimmers get into their rhythm on one stroke, they find themselves doing another. By the end, their lungs are bursting, and they are glad to touch the wall for the finish.

Relay Takeovers

1 *These swimmers are practising relay takeovers. The waiting swimmer had already started his dive when the incoming swimmer touched the wall. As long as his feet are still on the starting block when she touches, the takeover is legal.*

2 *If the waiting swimmer's feet had left the starting block before the other swimmer touched the wall, it would be called a 'flyer' or am 'illegal takeover'. The team would have been disqualified; mistiming a takeover can be a costly mistake!*

Swimmers thrash through the sea during a long-distance open-water swimming race.

Race Distances

Every stroke has races over 50m, 100m and 200m. The 50m races are flat-out sprints – 50m specialists need a lot of power, and very little endurance. The 100m and 200m racers need to combine speed with endurance. For front crawl swimmers, there are also freestyle races over 400m, 800m and 1500m.

Outside the pool, some swimmers specialize in open-water swimming, which takes place in the sea or lakes. Open-water competitions are swum over longer distances, for example 5km or 10km.

Relays

Relays are races in which four team-mates swim one after another. Relays are swum either freestyle or medley. In medley relays, the swimmers go in the order backstroke, breaststroke, butterfly, front crawl. Relays are usually 4x100m or 4x200m.

Record Holders

World Swimming Record Holders

	Men	Women
50m freestyle	Alexander Popov	Inge de Bruijn
100m freestyle	Pieter Van De Hoogenband	Britta Steffen
200m freestyle	Michael Phelps	Laure Manaudou
400m freestyle	Ian Thorpe	Laure Manaudou
800m freestyle	Grant Hackett	Janet Evans
1500m freestyle	Grant Hackett	Janet Evans
50m backstroke	Thomas Rupprath	Leila Vaziri
100m backstroke	Aaron Piersol	Natalie Coughlin
200m backstroke	Ryan Lochte	Krisztina Egerszegi
50m breaststroke	Oleg Lisogor	Jade Edmistone
100m breaststroke	Brendan Hansen	Leisel Jones
200m breaststroke	Brendan Hansen	Leisel Jones
50m butterfly	Roland Schoeman	Anna-Karin Kammerling
100m butterfly	Ian Crocker	Inge de Bruijn
200m butterfly	Michael Phelps	Jessicah Schipper
200m individual medley	Michael Phelps	Yanyan Wu
400m individual medley	Michael Phelps	Katie Hoff
Relays		
4x100m freestyle	U.S.A.	GERMANY
4x200m freestyle	U.S.A.	U.S.A.
4x100m medley	U.S.A	AUSTRALIA

Glossary

Bilateral breathing When a front-crawl swimmer turns his or her head both to the right and the left to breathe, instead of only on one side.

Disqualified Not allowed to take part, or not given a finishing place or a time.

Endurance The ability to carry on doing physical work or sport for a long time.

Flyer A swimmers' word that describes a false start (when someone starts too soon), or a too-quick takeover in a relay race.

Glide To move forwards through the water without effort or making a stroke.

Heats The first stage of a competition, when all the swimmers try to swim a fast enough time to make it into the semi-final or final.

Individual medley A race in which each swimmer does butterfly, backstroke, breaststroke and front crawl.

Lateral breathing When a front-crawl swimmer turns his or her head only to one side to breathe.

Long-distance In swimming, races of 400 metres or more.

Medley relay A race in which four swimmers in turn swim backstroke, breaststroke, butterfly and front crawl.

PB Short for 'personal best', the best time a swimmer has achieved in a particular event. For example, a swimmer might have PB of 55.72 for 100m freestyle. If he or she swims a time of 55.75, they would say they had got 'close to my PB'.

Professionals People who are paid for what they do are called professionals: a professional swimmer is paid to race.

Registration card The card a swimmer hands in at the start of a meet to let the officials know that he or she is there.

Relays Races where teams of four swimmers each swim in turn.

Sell-out An event where there are no tickets left because they have all been sold.

Sprint To go as fast as possible.

Streamlined Describes a shape that slides through air and water as easily as possible. A swimmer making a streamlined shape slides easily through the water.

Wall In swimming, a word that describes the end of the pool.

Websites

www.fina.org
The home website of the international governing body of swimming, with information about current swimmers, records, world rankings, and much more.

www.britishswimming.org
The home site of British swimming, with links to local clubs for people who want to learn to swim better, and to the Swim Active campaign that aims to encourage families to get fit through swimming.

www.swimmingworldmagazine.com
The latest news on what'shappening in the world of swimming, including interviews with current stars and latest results.

www.swimnews.com
Another news-based swimming site, with a strong international flavour.

Note to parents and teachers: every effort has been made by the Publishers to ensure that these websites are suitable for children, that they are of the highest educational value, and that they contain no inappropriate or offensive material. However, because of the nature of the Internet, it is impossible to guarantee that the contents of these sites will not be altered. We strongly advise that Internet access is supervised by a responsible adult.

Index